Good Habits for Happiness

To bring inner peace and contentment

for all your gift books and gift stationery

This edition first published in Great Britain in 2024
by Allsorted Ltd., WD19 4BG.

All rights reserved. No part of this work may be reproduced
in any form or by any means, electronic or mechanical,
including photocopying, recording or by any information
storage and retrieval system, without the prior written
permission of the publisher.

All information in this publication is for educational and
informational purposes. It is not intended as a substitute
for professional advice. Should you decide to act upon any
information in this publication, you do so at your own risk.
While the information in this publication has been verified to
the best of our abilities, we cannot guarantee that there are
no mistakes or errors.

© Susanna Geoghegan Gift Publishing

Author: Rebecca Dickinson

Illustrator: Jo Parry
Cover and concept design: Jo Parry and Nick Pettit
Contents design: Blackbird Brands

ISBN: 9-781-915902-53-5

Printed in China

10 9 8 7 6 5 4 3 2 1

Introduction

Happiness: The quality or condition of being happy.

Oxford English Dictionary

Happiness is a real gift that should be celebrated! It isn't all about having money, fame or acclaim; instead, a happy life is one that's filled with passion, purpose, positivity and pleasure, where you are the best version of yourself that you can possibly be.

In the midst of our busy lives, most of us can find practical and creative ways towards achieving greater happiness. So, if you're looking to put a spring in your step, increase the joy in your days and find greater meaning in your life, well, you've come to the right place. This book will take you by the hand and guide you towards a life you truly love.

Keep reading to discover the secrets of a fulfilling and meaningful life – and how to make these part of your daily routine in the pursuit of happiness …

*"Contentment
is the only
real wealth."*

Alfred Nobel

"Happiness depends upon ourselves."

Aristotle

What is happiness?

To be happy is to experience a state of positive well-being. Once our basic needs have been met, the desire for happiness is one that transcends languages, cultures, borders, religion, genders and wealth.

However, there's more to happiness than just having a good time. True happiness is a state of inner contentment and well-being that results from a sense of emotional balance and life satisfaction, which can be found in …

Pleasure
From eating delicious food, to seeing friends, to having sex, life's too short not to have fun! Taking part in pleasurable activities helps us to relax and boosts our happy hormones, like serotonin, dopamine and endorphins. But, as the effect is only temporary, we need other types of happiness, too.

Passion
Pursuing hobbies and interests gives us a sense of satisfaction, boosting our self-esteem. It can also help us to meet like-minded people and live a rich and varied life.

Purpose
This is about living in harmony with your values. Whether it's volunteering in the community, being part of a cause you care about, standing for political office, or bringing up children, knowing and following your purpose in life is vital to long-term happiness and fulfilment.

"Happiness is when
what you think,
what you say,
and what you do
are in harmony."

Mahatma Gandhi

Happiness myths

It can be easy to think that happiness looks like:

- a dream holiday
- a flashy car
- designer clothes
- a beautiful home
- flawless skin and a model figure
- a six-figure following on social media
- a salary the size of a small country's GDP.

But don't believe everything you read in magazines or watch on YouTube. There's no doubt that achieving our goals, or buying new things, can give us a buzz. This kind of happiness can be nice while it lasts – but it never does.

Studies show that while positive events – a romance, a new home, promotion –can produce a surge of joy, we start to adapt to the new status quo and quickly return to our original level of happiness, only to pursue another pleasure. Psychologists call this the 'hedonic treadmill' – and if you've ever been on a treadmill, you'll know that they don't really go anywhere …

Take winning the lottery, for example. Now, you might be interested to know that becoming an overnight millionaire isn't all it's cracked up to be. A number of studies show that landing a significant sum of money doesn't have any lasting impact on the winner's happiness.

So, if money can't buy us happiness, what can?

> ✶ ✶ ✶ ✶ **SPOILER ALERT** ✶ ✶ ✶ ✶
> You won't find it on Amazon or Instagram.

"Money can't buy happiness because happiness is not for sale."

Unknown

Happiness
is a journey,
not a
destination."

Unknown

Step off the treadmill

So, while winning the lottery — or buying a new car or a designer handbag — can bring about an initial high, our levels of happiness can soon revert to where they were before. This is known as 'hedonic adaptation'. It means that after experiencing positive events, we quickly adapt our expectations and return to our emotional baseline.*

But what if you could adjust that baseline? What if you could increase that underlying, set level of happiness? Well, the great news is, you can! Our individual levels of happiness are not fixed and unchangeable!

Long-term, sustainable happiness isn't a matter of fireworks and fanfares, it's a case of dialling up that emotional baseline.

And you can do that by building mood-boosting, positive habits: simple, regular activities that improve your overall well-being.

* Fortunately, the reverse is also true. Humans have an incredible capacity to demonstrate extraordinary resilience in the face of negative events and even to recover from the most terrible experiences.

"Happiness is a place between too much and too little."

Finnish proverb

"I have chosen to be happy because it is good for my health."

Voltaire

The foundations of happiness

The happiness we experience in our lives doesn't just come from the things that happen to us – although, of course, external events do play their part! Research suggests that around 10% of our happiness is determined by these events, while another 50% is down to our genetic make-up. That means that 40% is down to you!

Our capacity as humans to find and increase the levels of happiness in our lives is remarkable. Engaging in modest happiness-building habits and behaviours has a huge impact on our lives. Here are a few things that we can all do to benefit ourselves and those around us!

- Find pleasure in the little things – a walk in nature or time with family.

- Spend time with friends – celebrate the good times together and provide support during the bad.

- Nurture close relationships.

- Take care of your body and maintain your physical health.

- Look after your mental health – it's vital for your quality of life.

- Have meaningful experiences to enable you to learn more about yourself and reflect on what is important in your life.

- Explore hobbies, passions and interests – go and try something new!

- Carve out time for rest and relaxation.

"Most folks are as happy as they make up their minds to be."

Abraham Lincoln

"I, not events, have the power to make me happy or unhappy today. I can choose which it shall be. Yesterday is dead, tomorrow hasn't arrived yet. I have just one day, today, and I'm going to be happy in it."

Groucho Marx

The benefits of happiness

Happiness encompasses a range of emotions – from bouncing off the walls with joy, to a general sense of satisfaction, and everything in between. For most people, the bouncing off the walls bit isn't sustainable 24/7; it's the everything in between that counts!

Happiness isn't just a feeling, it's a way of life that brings some very positive benefits.

- **Happiness is great for your health:** It's the best form of medical insurance there is!

- **Happy people are more productive:** It's easier to be focused and get more done when you are happy and your life is in balance.

- **Happy people are more resilient:** They find it easier to cope with challenges and difficult situations, and are less likely to buckle under pressure.

- **Happiness strengthens relationships:** Happy people have more durable relationships with those around them. They are able to be a better friend/sister/brother/partner.

- **When you are happy, others want to be around you:** You will have a great social life!

- **Happiness boosts self-esteem:** Happy people are confident in themselves and their abilities.

- **Happy people notice the positives rather than the negatives:** They find joy in unexpected places.

- **Happiness is contagious:** If you are happy, you will make other people happier, too.

"For every minute you are angry, you lose sixty seconds of happiness."

Ralph Waldo Emerson

The power of optimism

If there's one trait that happy people have in common, it's optimism. They are the glass-half-full individuals who always seem to have something to smile about!

Optimism is a belief that life is likely to turn out well. It's true: some people are wired to look on the bright side, while others are natural-born pessimists. Having an optimistic mindset helps you to think and feel positively – and it bring extra benefits that will augment your levels of happiness, too.

- **You are less likely to get ill:** Studies suggest that optimism can reduce your risk of cancer, heart disease, stroke and infections. Unsurprisingly, research also shows that optimistic people live longer than pessimists.

- **Your mental health benefits:** Optimists are less likely to suffer from depression and anxiety.

- **You have more blessings to count:** Optimists don't just expect good things to happen, they actively take steps to make them happen!

- **You have greater confidence, resilience and self-esteem:** Optimists are more likely to believe in themselves and their ability to cope with bad events.

"You only live once,
but if you do it right,
once is enough."

Mae West

"The primary cause of unhappiness is never the situation, but your thoughts about it. Be aware of the thoughts you are thinking."

Eckhart Tolle

Overcoming the negativity bias

Although optimism is a key component of happiness, the human brain has developed over time to pay more attention to negative events than to positive ones.

This comes down to something called the 'negativity bias'. Thousands of years ago, our ancestors needed to be aware of dangers in their environment in order to stay alive. This meant their brains were programmed to look out for threats. Now, while those threats have substantially changed and society has moved on, our DNA hasn't. This means that everyday challenges can leave us stuck in 'fight or flight' mode, which can lead to chronic stress and anxiety.

However, by thinking positively and by developing and maintaining qualities like gratitude, kindness, optimism and relaxation, we can learn to overcome the negativity bias. Take time to enjoy – and savour – the positive moments that you feel, and build up a wealth of happy memories that you can reflect on and enjoy in the future!

In the words of the song …

> **You got to ac-cent-tchu-ate the positive**
>
> **E-lim-i-nate the negative**
>
> **Latch on to the affirmative**
>
> **Don't mess with Mr In-between."**

"Optimism is a strategy for making a better future. Because unless you believe that the future can be better, it's unlikely you will step up and take responsibility for making it so."

Noam Chomsky

"I am not afraid of storms,
for I am learning how
to sail my ship."

Louisa May Alcott

Count your blessings

Being thankful helps us to focus on the things we have, rather than the things we don't have. And scientific studies prove that practising gratitude makes us happier and healthier.

True gratitude isn't just a cursory thanks, a hasty merci, or an obligatory "much obliged", it involves acknowledging all the things that brighten your life or your day. Every day.

Make gratitude a habit! Here are some ways to celebrate the pluses in your life and to boost your levels of happiness.

- **Keep a gratitude journal:** Each night, before you go to sleep, write down three things you're grateful for. Not just the big things, but all the other stuff, too – rainbows, butterflies, buttered toast, your favourite jumper, great friends, good coffee, or just a warm bed to sleep in.

🍂 **Express it:** Is there someone in your life you're super-thankful for? Why not let them know with a heartfelt thank you? If you're feeling shy, you could write them a letter instead.

🍂 **Share it:** Telling people when you feel grateful can amplify those feelings and encourage others to notice the positive things in their lives, too.

"Be thankful for what you have; you'll end up having more. If you concentrate on what you don't have, you will never, ever have enough."

Oprah Winfrey

"Gratitude is riches.
Complaint is poverty."

Doris Day

Practise kindness

Kindness is powerful stuff. A reassuring hug or a helping hand can make the world of difference when you're having a hard time. But kindness works both ways. Studies show that doing something nice for others also boosts your own mood. It's a win–win.

You don't need to give away all your worldly possessions; often, it's the little things that mean the most and have the greatest impact. Here are some ways to be kind and spread a little happiness.

- Pay someone a compliment – don't forget to make eye contact and smile to show that you mean it.

- Cook a meal for someone who has been unwell or is feeling down or lonely.

- Give away something you no longer need.

- Leave a positive review for a small business.

- Catch up with someone you haven't seen for a while.

- Offer to look after a tired parent's children for a night or a weekend.

- Surprise a friend with a homemade cake.

- Pay for a stranger's coffee – or even their shopping (if you are able).

- Put out your neighbour's recycling.

And don't forget to be kind to yourself, too!

"Those who bring sunshine into the lives of others cannot keep it from themselves."

James M. Barrie

Find your meaning

Studies show that having meaningful experiences is one of the key elements of long-term happiness. Finding your meaning goes beyond pleasure; it's about doing things that fit with your personal beliefs and values.

Meaningful activities provide a sense of fulfilment and purpose that contribute to your overall well-being and happiness. These should be celebrated! They help you to feel connected to something beyond yourself, and might include:

- working on a cause that's close to your heart
- contributing to your community
- making a positive impact on the planet.

Use the following questions to help you focus on rewarding ways that may help you make a difference in the world.

- If you could change one thing in the world, what would it be?

- How would you like to make an impact on society?

- How would you most like to be remembered?

- Who inspires you?

- What makes you feel fulfilled?

- What do you believe in?

- What is a dream you have always had?

"The privilege of a
lifetime is to become
who you truly are."

C.G. Jung

"Be like an elephant:
Remember what matters,
look out for your herd,
and don't be afraid to
take up space."

Lori Deschene

Sleep well

If there's one habit that underpins every aspect of our physical and mental health, it's sleep. Your life literally depends upon it! For optimum well-being – and to have you springing out of bed in the morning – try to get at least seven hours every night. As boring as it sounds, the key is to go to bed at the same time every night and to get up at the same time every morning. Here are some of the benefits.

- **Your mood will improve:** Sleep affects the amygdala, the deep emotional control centre of the brain. A good night's sleep will help to restore your emotional equilibrium.

- **Sleep helps to keeps sniffles at bay:** During sleep, the immune system carries out important work fighting infection. Sleep also gives the body a chance to repair muscles and tissues, and to replace worn-out cells.

- **Sleep protects us from serious illnesses:** Evidence shows that sleep reduces the risk of numerous conditions, including diabetes, heart disease, Alzheimer's and even cancer.

- **Sleep can help you stay slim:** Sleep deprivation messes with levels of leptin and ghrelin in the body – the hormones that control appetite. This means you're more likely to overeat after a rough night.

- **You'll get better results:** Sleep improves memory, learning and concentration.

"The best bridge between despair and hope is a good night's sleep."

E. Joseph Cossman

"Sleep is that golden chain that ties health and our bodies together."

Thomas Dekker

Get up with the sun

The jury is firmly in: exposure to early-morning sunlight brightens your mood.

It's not just the act of getting up and moving. Exposing yourself to sunlight first thing helps regulate your body clock, or circadian rhythm, helping you to feel more alert. It also increases your level of serotonin, which boosts your mood and helps regulate your emotions.

Here are some more good reasons to get outdoors before breakfast.

- Early morning light can enhance your mood throughout the day, not just first thing.

- Natural light plays an important role in setting your body clock. This helps you to sleep better at night.

- A lack of sun exposure is linked to low levels of serotonin, which can lead to seasonal depression (formerly known as 'seasonal affective disorder' or 'SAD') – a type of depression triggered by the changing seasons.

- Even on a cloudy winter's day, daylight still provides better light than indoor lighting.

- Sunlight also boosts your vitamin D levels.

- You'll be able to give yourself a pat on the back for resisting the snooze button.

"Lose an hour in the morning, and you will be all day hunting for it."

Richard Whately

"There was never
a night or a problem
that could defeat
sunrise or hope."

Bernard Williams

Try savouring

The expression 'savour the moment' is all about living fully in the present; noticing and enjoying moments of beauty and pleasure, and appreciating what you have. It's an effective way to improve your quality of life.

Whether it's a spectacular sunset or a delicious bowl of soup, paying attention to enjoyable experiences – however trivial they may seem – encourages us to focus on the positive, which sets us up for long-lasting happiness.

Try these tips for savouring …

- **Use all your senses:** For example, if you're eating something you love, notice how it smells, looks, and feels in your mouth, as well as how it tastes.

- **Slow. Down:** In our hectic world, it's so easy to rush from one thing to the next. The next time you're tempted to whizz through a pleasurable moment, try stretching it out to prolong and intensify your enjoyment.

- **Reduce distractions:** It's impossible to fully appreciate an experience when your attention is being pulled in several directions at once. So, turn off screens when eating, leave your phone at home – or put it on silent – when going for a walk, and never take it to bed.

"To live in the moment ...

is the only footprint

one must follow."

Oglala Lakota–Hinhan Wakangli

"My number one daily habit is to give myself permission to be happy."

Michelle Obama

The power of relationships

Human beings have an innate need to connect with other human beings. So, it's no surprise that having strong relationships is one of the most important components of happiness.

Our close friends and family provide us with a sense of belonging, security and support. They are the people we turn to in times of need and in times of joy. And, in return, we can be a source of support to them.

Numerous studies show that strong social connections are vital to our physical and mental health and well-being. In fact, research proves that the happiest people are the people with close, supportive friendships and relationships.

All relationships go through ups and downs, but it's important to invest time and energy to nurture and maintain happy, healthy connections with the people you love. These recommendations will help you to develop strong and resilient relationships.

- Communicate honestly and openly.
- Listen attentively.
- Express your appreciation.
- Work through differences.
- Apologise when necessary.
- Share household chores.
- Spend quality time together.
- Have fun together.

"Let us be grateful to the people who make us happy; they are the charming gardeners who make our souls blossom."

Marcel Proust

Get connected

There's no substitute for meeting people in 'real life', but used in the right way, social media can facilitate actual relationships and help combat loneliness. So, rather than trawling through other people's perfectly curated lives on Facebook, these apps may be a more worthwhile way of finding long-lasting connections and celebrating relationships in all their forms.

- **Meetup:** Free this Friday evening? Meetup is an app that lists events and clubs in your area so you can connect with people who share your interests.

- **Bumble For Friends:** Like a dating app, only for friendship. This one will match you up with like-minded people.

- **Hey! VINA:** This is another friendship app that aims to empower and connect females around the world. Think: Tinder for girls.

🍂 **Nextdoor:** Want to get to know your neighbours but not brave enough to knock on doors? Join Nextdoor – the international app that brings communities together.

🍂 **Peanut:** From having a baby, to navigating the menopause, Peanut is an app that connects women who are going through the same stage of life.

🍂 **Yubo:** Targeted at teenagers, this site aims to provide a safe platform for young people to discover new friends.

"There is no hope
of joy except in
human relations."

Antoine de Saint-Exupéry

"A day without a friend
is like a pot without
a single drop of
honey left inside."

Winnie the Pooh

Positive affirmations

A positive affirmation is a short phrase, or mantra, with an uplifting or inspiring message that is designed to help you change your life forever. You could write your affirmations on Post-it notes and stick them on a wall, a mirror or somewhere else you will easily see them. Or you could recite them out loud. The louder the better!

Repeating positive affirmations can help overcome negative thoughts and bring about a change in your internal voice that will ultimately lead to a more positive outlook and help you to feel more empowered. Repeating affirmations that are relevant to you is a great way to motivate yourself – and the more you repeat an affirmation, the sooner you'll start to believe it.

Here are some examples:

- I matter.
- I am relevant.
- I choose happiness.
- I am not defined by my past.
- Things can only get better.
- I am strong.
- I am special and unique.
- I am in control of my own destiny.
- I deserve good things.
- I am a survivor.

Try to create some affirmations of your own – keep them positive and personal, and you'll see how they can buoy you up and give you greater confidence.

"No one can steal contentment, joy, gratitude, or peace – we have to give it away."

Kristin Armstrong

"The world is full of people looking for spectacular happiness while they snub contentment."

Doug Larson

Try a mindfulness exercise

In today's fast-paced world, we all need to find a moment of calm now and then; doing a mindfulness exercise is a great way to achieve this. Mindfulness is the simple act of paying attention to the present moment. This helps to quieten the noise in our minds and enables us to find greater enjoyment in life.

One of the easiest ways to practise mindfulness is simply to focus on your breath. Find somewhere quiet, and sit in a comfortable position. Now, notice your breath as it flows in and out of your body. Don't try to force it – just relax and observe it.

Another technique is to focus on an everyday object, such as an apple, a glass or a leaf. Hold the object in your hands and use all your senses to examine it, giving it your full attention. If you become distracted by other thoughts, just acknowledge them and let them go, then return to your mindfulness.

Try to practise mindfulness for a few minutes every day – or whenever you feel overwhelmed – until it becomes a habit. This provides a useful antidote to worrying about the future or stressing about the past. Notice how it improves your happiness and well-being.

"You don't have to control your thoughts. You just have to stop letting them control you."

Dan Millman

"Turn your face toward the sun and the shadows will fall behind you."

Māori proverb

Seven reasons to be creative

There is a strong relationship between creativity and happiness. Creative activities allow us to forget about our worries and provide a sense of fulfilment. From painting, to pottery, to piano-playing, you don't have to be talented, you just have to get stuck in.

- Creative hobbies trigger the brain to release dopamine, a natural antidepressant.

- They also help us to understand ourselves and to express our emotions.

- Having a creative interest prevents boredom. Practising a creative hobby improves problem-solving skills, which improves resilience. This benefits other areas of life, too.

- Creativity requires focus, which improves concentration.

- Getting lost in a creative activity can lead to a state of flow, where you feel happy and energised.

- Having a creative hobby can lead to unexpected opportunities. They can be a way of socialising with like-minded people, or be the start of a successful business idea – you could start to sell your creations, such as clothes, greetings cards, artwork, baked goods or jewellery. Or you could give them away as presents.

Not sure what to try? Here are a few ideas you might enjoy …

- Origami
- Flower-arranging or making wreaths
- Repurposing old clothing or furniture
- Making skincare products
- Candle-making
- Basket-making
- Poetry-writing
- Doodling or cartooning
- Lego

"A creative life is an amplified life. It's a bigger life, a happier life, an expanded life, and a hell of a lot more interesting life."

Elizabeth Gilbert

Find your spark

When life is a conveyor belt of responsibilities and obligations, it can be easy to neglect the things we love. But making time for activities you truly enjoy is an essential component of happiness.

We all have things that ignite our spark. These are the activities that make us feel joyful, energised and alive. It doesn't matter how talented or accomplished you are, finding your spark isn't about winning medals or achieving recognition; it's about making time for the things that feed your soul and help you experience that blissful state of flow, where you are so absorbed in what you are doing that you lose track of time and place.

So what ignites your spark? It could be a sport, a creative hobby, a musical passion, a craft, or an environmental or spiritual pursuit.

If you are looking to find that special something that drives you, ask yourself the following questions.

- What makes you feel excited?

- What are you most passionate about?

- What makes you joyful?

- What would you like to do more of?

- What motivates you?

"Whatever you do, always give 100%. Unless you're donating blood."

Bill Murray

"Don't compromise yourself – you're all you have."

Lori Deschene

Breathe well

We all have times when life's ups and down send us out of kilter and we need to feel more in control. Breathing exercises are a useful tool when you feel stressed, anxious or just need some time out to restore your emotional balance. To really benefit from these exercises, it is important to breathe into your tummy, rather than your chest. This is called 'abdominal breathing' – or 'belly breathing' – and it stimulates the vagus nerve, which helps us to feel relaxed, safe and calm.

Try these techniques
Lie on your back, or sit in a comfortable position, then place one hand on your upper chest and the other on your abdomen, just below your ribcage. Breathe in through your nose and let your abdomen rise; your chest should stay fairly still. Then breathe out through your mouth, noticing how your abdomen flattens as you exhale.

Once you feel comfortable with abdominal breathing, try the following calming breath technique.

- Breathe in deeply through your nose for a count of four.

- Hold your breath for a count of seven.

- Exhale through your mouth for a count of eight, as if slowly blowing out a candle.

- Repeat the cycle a few more times.

"For breath is life, and if you breathe well you will live long on Earth."

Sanskrit proverb

"When you own your breath, nobody can steal your peace."

Unknown

Nourish your body

"You are what you eat," goes the saying. The food we put in our bodies has a huge impact on our physical and mental well-being.

Life is too short never to eat a biscuit – and however good our usual food choices, we all need a treat now and then – but the constant onslaught of fad diets and nutritional brainwashing can make healthy eating seem like a minefield.

However, if there's one simple habit we could all adopt that will benefit our bodies and minds, it's this: eat more real food. In other words: eat fewer ultra-processed foods (UPFs). These are foods that tend to contain ingredients only used in the food industry, such as preservatives, emulsifiers and sweeteners. This diverse group of foods includes:

- packaged snacks, such as biscuits and pastries
- most supermarket-bought bread and wraps

- breakfast cereals and cereal bars
- ham and other processed meats
- flavoured yogurts
- ready meals, such as pizzas and pasta sauces containing preservatives, emulsifiers, sweeteners and artificial colours and flavours.

Despite their prevalence, recent research proves UPFs increase the risk of cancer, heart disease, stroke, obesity and poor mental health. And while we might not be able to avoid them completely, cutting back could make the world of difference to your health and happiness. Try to eat more natural foods, or foods that have been through less processing.

> ********** TIP **********
> Always read the label and try to avoid ingredients you wouldn't find in your own kitchen.

"Those who think they have no time for healthy eating will sooner or later have to find time for illness."

Edward Stanley

"Your diet is a

bank account.

Good food choices

are good

investments."

Bethenny Frankel

Brighten up your life

Colours can have a really positive effect on your well-being. While painting your bedroom a new shade of fuchsia, or dressing up like Barbie, might not solve all your problems, it could give you a brighter outlook. Certain colours are known to have an impact on mood, stress levels and general well-being.

Dopamine dressing – dressing for happiness – can help you to look good and feel great! Even adding pops of colour to an outfit with statement accessories can make you feel more confident. When it comes to your home, you don't have to paint the whole house; a few colourful soft furnishings could do the trick. It's out with the beige and in with the rainbow. Find the joy in using colour!

Get the vibes

 Reds and oranges: These bold, bright colours can help you feel more confident. They can also make you appear stronger to other people.

- **Green:** The colour of nature is said to bring calm and balance.

- **Yellow:** Warm colours, like mustard and sunset, are thought to increase alertness and energy levels.

- **Blues:** Shades such as sky blue have a calming energy that promotes relaxation.

"I found I could say things with color and shapes that I couldn't say any other way."

Georgia O'Keeffe

"Color is a power which directly influences the soul."

Wassily Kandinksy

Choose to move

We all know how important it is to stay active. Regular exercise is great for your physical health but it also comes with a wide range of other benefits – from improving sleep quality, to boosting self-esteem and increasing happiness.

Here are just a few good reasons to keep exercising.

- **It's a natural anti-depressant:** Exercise causes your body to release 'happy' chemicals like serotonin and endorphins, which can relieve the symptoms of mild to moderate depression.

- **It can reduce stress and anxiety:** Physical activity distracts you from worries and negative thoughts, leading to a more positive frame of mind. It can also help relieve muscle tension brought on by stress.

- **It helps you focus:** Exercise boosts hormones that support memory, motivation and concentration.

- **It's a great icebreaker:** Exercising with others can open new social doors.

- **It boosts self-esteem:** Exercise leads to progress, which leads to confidence, which helps you to feel good about yourself.

- **It strengthens your bones and muscles:** Strong bones and muscles are especially important as you get older.

- **It's maths:** Being active helps you live longer. Regular exercise can reduce the chance of dying early from conditions like heart disease and cancer by around 30%. Aim for 150 minutes of activity per week.

"Physical fitness can neither be achieved by wishful thinking nor outright purchase."

Joseph Pilates

"A year from now
you may wish you
had started today."

Karen Lamb

Find an exercise that's right for you

You don't have to sign up for a marathon, train for a triathlon or scale a mountain to enjoy the benefits of exercise. Like people, sport comes in all shapes and sizes. The important thing is to find something that makes you happy and that you'll want to keep on doing!

Here are a few ideas to help you stay physically active.

- **Rollerbooting:** The 1980s are back, and you'll be having so much fun you won't even realise you're keeping fit. (Knee pads and helmet recommended!)

- **Skateboarding:** Now an Olympic sport – what more incentive do you need?

- **Martial arts:** Work up a sweat and learn how to defend yourself at the same time. It's a win–win.

- **Online workouts:** Don't fancy the gym? YouTube is full of free-to-access fitness classes. No one will ever know you're still in your pyjamas.

- **Walk or cycle to work or school:** Avoid traffic and travel expenses while getting in some steps. Working from home? Take a walking lunchbreak or take phone calls on the move.

- **Stand-up paddleboarding:** There's a reason this is one of the fastest-growing sports on the planet – and not just because it's great for your core. Give it a try, and find out for yourself.

"Pain is temporary.

Quitting lasts forever."

Lance Armstrong

"Fitness is not about being better than someone else. It's about being better than you used to be."

Khloe Kardashian

Bump up your vitamin D

Soaking up some rays is the best way to ensure you're getting enough vitamin D. The so-called 'sunshine vitamin' is created by the body from the direct action of sunlight on the skin. This essential vitamin helps to regulate the amount of calcium and phosphate in the body, which helps to keep bones, teeth and muscles healthy, and may also support the immune system.

Vitamin D can also make you happier! Low levels of the vitamin have been linked to depression and anxiety, so in addition to the mood-boosting effects of simply being outdoors, getting out in the sunshine will help to keep your levels topped up.

In countries like the UK, there isn't enough sunlight during the winter for the body to produce enough vitamin D, so it's a good idea to take a supplement between October and March. You could also try including sources of vitamin D in your diet.

These foods all provide some vitamin D.

- Oily fish, such as salmon, sardines and mackerel
- Red meat
- Liver
- Egg yolks
- Mushrooms
- Fortified milks and cereals

"It is only possible to live happily ever after on a daily basis."

Margaret Bonanno

Embrace *Oubaitori*

It's natural to compare ourselves with other people – but that doesn't mean it's always helpful. Everyone is different and we should celebrate that!

Oubaitori (pronounced: oh-buy-toe-ree) is a Japanese principle inspired by flowers. It's a beautifully simple illustration of the way in which we are all on our own journey through life.

In Japanese, the word *Oubaitori* is written as 桜梅桃李. The four characters represent the four trees that bloom in spring: cherry, apricot, peach and plum. Each flower blossoms at a different time and in a different colour, eventually going on to produce delicious fruit. No flower or tree is better or worse than another. They all enhance the landscape without noticing what the others are doing.

Oubaitori applies this concept to people, explaining how we all travel our own unique path through life. We all blossom and grow in our own way, at our own pace. So, the next time you're tempted to compare yourself to someone else, remember: a cherry tree is not a peach tree, and you, too, are on your path, with your own wonderful strengths and unique qualities.

> "Comparison is the thief of joy."

Theodore Roosevelt

"Don't compare yourself to others. There's no comparison between the sun and the moon. They shine when it's their time."

Unknown

Look for glimmers

You are probably already familiar with the term 'trigger' – something that provokes negative or unwanted memories. But what about the opposite? That's right: a 'glimmer'. Glimmers are small cues that ignite a sense of joy or peace – and these tiny moments can be a great boost to your mood and help you to feel calm and secure.

Whereas triggers tend to throw us into a state of 'fight or flight', glimmers do the exact opposite, by sending an 'I'm safe' message to the nervous system. As well as sparking a moment of happiness, glimmers help us to feel 'in the moment'. So, instead of stressing about the future or agonising over the past, glimmers encourage us to notice – and enjoy – the present.

It can be easy to rush past the simple, seemingly insignificant, moments in our day – the scent of flowers, the sound of birdsong, feeling the sun on your face – but while they may be tiny, noticing and appreciating glimmers can be a small step to living more mindfully and contentedly. Let glimmers into your life and delight in the moments of happiness they can evoke.

"Always be on the lookout for the presence of wonder."

E.B. White

"To see a World in a Grain of Sand

And a Heaven in a Wild Flower

Hold Infinity in the palm of your hand

And Eternity in an hour."

William Blake

Unplug

Technology can be a huge asset to modern life; we can watch movies, order food, work from home, and communicate with friends and family around the world – all thanks to our devices. But those same devices can also be a huge source of stress and distraction. From the way we work, to the way we interact, many of us spend hours of each day on our screens – and we can sometimes be overwhelmed by a frenzy of emails, notifications, pings, bleeps and whooshes.

Completely eliminating all forms of technology probably isn't possible, or practical, for most of us. But there are huge benefits to be gained from taking a regular digital detox. For example, you could decide to turn off devices at a set time every day. Or you could try screen-free Sundays.

Here are some reasons to unplug.

- It helps create boundaries between your home and work life.
- It allows you to appreciate the beauty of quietness.
- It allows for mental relaxation and rejuvenation.
- You'll sleep better.
- It gives you the chance to focus on real relationships – and yourself.
- It gives you the space to just enjoy living in the present moment.

"Real connection

happens in the

real world."

Unknown

"LIFE IS WHAT HAPPENS WHEN YOU PUT YOUR PHONE AWAY."

Unknown

Accept all your emotions

Happiness is awesome. But let's face it: nobody, not even the happiest person on the planet, feels happy all the time.

We get bad news, we mess up, people hurt us, families make us mad, we get scared, stuff goes wrong. Sometimes, very wrong. In other words: life happens. And while having a positive attitude can make a huge difference to how we react to life's ups and downs, it's important not to gloss over problems or to deny our true feelings. All emotions – including grief, anger, sadness and disgust – play an important role in our lives. And when they pass, they can help us to truly appreciate feelings of happiness even more.

When you're having a hard day or a hard month, acknowledge that you are feeling unhappy. Allow yourself the space to think about why you are feeling this way and what might help.

Look after your physical needs, lean on others for support, take time out, try spending time in nature, if you can, and never be ashamed to seek professional help if your feelings are too powerful for you to handle alone.

*** REMEMBER ***
This too will pass.

"It's up to us to choose contentment and thankfulness now – and to stop imagining that we have to have everything perfect before we'll be happy."

Joanna Gaines

"There is no end of craving. Hence contentment alone is the best way to happiness. Therefore, acquire contentment."

Swami Sivananda

Positive thoughts for difficult days

Your mental health is just as important as your physical health, yet it can still be hard to talk about. However, looking after your emotional and psychological well-being, and seeking support when necessary, helps change the way you think, feel and behave. This will also have a positive effect on your relationships, your work life, your confidence and your self-esteem, leading to a greater sense of happiness and well-being.

When you are in need of extra support, be kind to yourself – and remember …

- It's okay not to be okay.

- Your condition does not define you.

- A mental illness is not a weakness, it's a medical condition.

- There is no stigma in taking medication for a mental health condition.
- You have the power to manage your mental health.
- However long or winding the journey, healing is possible.
- It's fine to say no to things or to take time out when you're feeling overwhelmed.
- You are capable of living a fulfilling life.
- You are worthy of love.
- You deserve peace of mind.
- You deserve happiness.

"And still I rise."

Maya Angelou

"Happiness can be found
even in the darkest of times,
if one only remembers
to turn on the light."

Albus Dumbledore (J.K. Rowling)

Sort your stuff out

Whether you live in a tiny flat or a sprawling mansion, your physical environment can have a huge impact on your well-being. You might not be able to afford a new house – or even a new kitchen – but you can sort out the one you have!

Decluttering is a great way to increase your levels of happiness; it helps you feel calmer and more in control, and it allows you to work out what's important to you.

Here are some more perks.

- **It can help your relationships:** Living in a disorderly home can lead to arguments and resentment over whose turn it is to do the chores. When everyone does their bit, harmony follows.

- 🍂 **It keeps bugs at bay:** A messy home can be a breeding ground for bacteria, or worse – unwelcome house guests such as mice or moths.

- 🍂 **Brighter mornings:** An ordered home means no more hunting for your keys under a pile of junk mail. It's so much easier to find things when everything has its place!

- 🍂 **Better nights:** A tidy bedroom is much more conducive to sleep than a messy one.

- 🍂 **You could be better off:** Selling unwanted clothes and other items, for example on online auction sites, frees up space and could make you some cash.

"The objective of cleaning is not just to clean, but to feel happiness living within that environment."

Marie Kondo

"Clutter is not just the stuff on your floor, it's anything that stands between you and the life you want to be living."

Peter Walsh

Just dance

Dancing is a fantastic full-body workout. But it's not just about the calories; shaking your booty is a great way to feel happier, too.

The combination of music and movement stimulates reward centres in the brain, giving you a double hit of pleasure. Whether you're a prima ballerina or have two left feet, dancing has the power to make you feel good.

So, why not …

- **Sign up for a class:** Whether or not you danced as a child, there are dance classes for all ages and abilities.

- **Find a style that suits you:** Not keen on ballet or ballroom? There are dance styles to suit all tastes. Belly dancing, burlesque, flamenco, street dance, hip-hop – there really is something for everyone!

- **Dance your way to fitness:** Try a dance workout, such as Zumba.

- **Create a dance playlist:** Freestyle your way around the kitchen!

- **Check out the latest trends online:** If the thought of joining a class fills you with dread, there are countless dances on TikTok and YouTube. Or try an app like Just Dance Now.

"I do not try to dance better than anyone else. I only try to dance better than myself."

Mikhail Baryshnikov

Just sing

Like dancing, singing is an incredible way to boost your happiness and well-being. Research shows that people feel happier and more positive after singing out loud than they do when just listening to music.

Besides being hugely beneficial for your mood, singing also improves breathing, posture and muscle tension. There's even evidence to suggest it can improve your immune system by decreasing levels of the stress hormone cortisol. In addition, singing with others is a great bonding experience and a way of getting out there and meeting new people.

Even if you don't think you are musically gifted, it's thought that most people have some musical ability. So, what are you waiting for?

- **Join a choir:** If a church choir isn't your thing, then how about a rock or pop choir? Thousands of people have already discovered the benefits.

- **Try karaoke:** Pop along to a karaoke night, or hold your own.

- **Create a playlist of upbeat, happy songs:** And sing your heart out.

- **Sing in the shower:** What a great way to start the day! And if you're feeling really brave ... Audition for a show like *The X Factor*.

"Those who wish to sing always find a song."

Swedish proverb

"Words make you think.

Music makes you feel.

A song makes you feel

a thought."

E.Y. Harburg

Get cosy

Light some candles and cuddle up with a hot water bottle. *Hygge* (pronounced: hue-gah) is a Danish word and it roughly translates as a feeling of cosiness and well-being.

Despite its long, cold winters, Denmark is ranked as one of the happiest countries in the world. And it seems *hygge* has a lot to do with it. This Scandinavian tradition involves basking in a warm, homely atmosphere – especially when it's cold and dark outside.

But there's more to *hygge* than just sheepskin rugs, fluffy socks and hot chocolate (as lovely as these things are). True *hygge* isn't a hashtag, it's a state of mind; a feeling of inner comfort and contentedness that leaves you feeling warm on both the outside and the inside.

Embracing hygge involves letting go of your worries and relaxing in the present moment. It's about focusing on your well-being and connecting with yourself, your environment and the people around you. So shut the curtains, put the kettle on, string up some fairy lights (if you like) and snuggle up. Ah, bliss.

"One of the secrets
of a happy life
is continuous
small treats ..."

Iris Murdoch

"The happiness of life is made up of minute fractions – the little, soon-forgotten charities of a kiss, a smile, a kind look … and the countless other infinitesimals of pleasant thought and genial feeling."

Samuel Taylor Coleridge

Have more sex

We all know that sex and pleasure go hand in hand. But science proves that sex isn't just enjoyable, it's good for you, too. And you don't even need a partner to reap the benefits.

Intimate stimulation causes a surge in feel-good hormones, promoting mental and physical health. What's more, during climax, the amygdala – the region of the brain associated with fear and anxiety – is blocked, further enhancing that feeling of well-being.

As well as feeling great, regular orgasms can also reduce pain and boost the immune system, helping to stave off infections. For women, orgasms have the added benefit of toning the pelvic floor muscles. And for men, regular ejaculation may lower the risk of prostate cancer.

Sex between couples strengthens relationships, but if you don't have a partner, you can enjoy the benefits of orgasm through self-love. And if you've ever needed an excuse to invest in an adult toy, you might like to know that vibrators were first designed for medical reasons, including to treat 'hysteria'.

"Sex is a part of nature.
I go along with nature."

Marilyn Monroe

"Girl power is about
loving yourself and having
confidence and strength
from within, so even
if you're not wearing a
sexy outfit, you feel sexy."

Nicole Scherzinger

Crack a smile

Smiling is like wearing your happiness on the outside — like a cheerful scarf or a bright necklace. It's a universally recognised sign that tells people we are happy. But it can work both ways: smiling doesn't just show we are happy, it can actually make us happier, too.

It's all down to something called the 'facial feedback hypothesis'. The idea is that our emotional experiences are influenced by our facial expressions. So, smiling should make us feel happier – although, of course, the reverse is also true!

A genuine smile reaches your cheeks and eyes, not just the corners of your mouth. This is known as a 'Duchenne smile'. If you're not in a smiley mood, thinking of something pleasant, or funny, or even a little bit cheeky and putting on a smile may help to elevate your mood. And because smiling is contagious, your smile may help to brighten up someone else's day, too.

> * * * * * * * * **TRY THIS** * * * * * * * *
> Smile at yourself in the mirror each morning and see if it helps get your day off to a good start.

"Not what we have, but what we enjoy, constitutes our abundance."

Epicurus

Get outdoors more

Spending time in the great outdoors is one of the best ways to boost your happiness. Masses of research shows that being in nature helps keep depression and anxiety at bay, and can even provide a 'protective zone' that goes beyond the powers of medication.

There's no need to head for the hills – unless, of course, you want to. A green space can be anywhere nature is allowed to thrive: a local park, your own backyard, a rooftop garden or a balcony.

Here are some more ways to connect with nature.

- Spend a day at a nature reserve.

- Visit a bird or wildlife sanctuary.

- Visit a city farm.

- Get involved with a community garden or school gardening project.

- Spend a morning at a pick-your-own farm.

- Start a vegetable patch – if you don't have any outdoor space, many vegetables can be grown in pots outside, or even on a windowsill.

- Go on a camping trip.

- Join a local walking group.

- Make a bug house.

- Hang up a bird feeder.

"A walk in nature walks the soul back home."

Mary Davis

"The Poetry of earth

is never dead …"

John Keats

Find some blue space

So, we know that green spaces are great for well-being. But what about blue spaces? Yes, we're talking rivers, lakes, oceans, canals, muddy puddles. Okay, maybe not puddles, but anywhere else there's a natural body of water.

Here are some watery facts.

- Before birth, we spend our formative months in watery amniotic fluid.

- Our bodies are about 60% water.

- The Earth's surface is made up of around 71% water.

It seems only natural, then, that we should have a deep affinity with the stuff that surrounds us and keeps us – and our planet – alive. Recent research supports this, showing that being in or near blue spaces, such as rivers, lakes and the sea, leads to greater happiness and emotional well-being. In fact, some experts now believe that blue spaces could be even more beneficial than green ones.

Some of the benefits that marine environments can bring include:

- better mood.
- reduced anxiety.
- improved sleep.
- improved clarity and decision-making.

"Ocean separates lands,

not souls."

Munia Khan

"The ocean stirs the heart, inspires the imagination and brings eternal joy to the soul."

Louisa May Alcott

Spend time around water

There is something special, almost mystical, about marine environments: still water promotes feelings of inner peace and well-being; rushing rivers stimulate the senses; wild coastlines inspire and invigorate us; and sunny beaches can invoke happy memories of childhood and summer holidays.

Wherever you live, spending more time in, or near, water can have a powerful influence on your mental and physical health. Research has shown that being close to water can have an impact on transmitters in the brain that affect mood; it can bring you to a calmer, more meditative state and can encourage creativity.

Here are some ways to catch the buzz!

- Gaze at a glassy lake.
- Watch a cascading waterfall.

- Breathe in the scent of the ocean.
- Wander beside a canal.
- Sit, or stroll, beside a rushing river.
- Listen to the sound of a trickling stream.
- Trail your fingers in a fountain.
- Observe the gentle ebb and flow of the tide.
- Marvel at the power of crashing waves.
- Take a walk on a wild, empty beach.
- Lie on warm sand.
- Take a swim!

"A calm water is like a still soul."

Lailah Gifty Akita

"All water is holy water."

Rajiv Joseph

Take a moment to relax

We all have moments when life gets on top of us. When that happens, our muscles soon tense up. Try this simple exercise to help release physical tension.

Start by getting into a comfortable position, either lying or sitting down.

- First, take a few slow, deep breaths into your abdomen, so that your belly rises but your shoulders stay where they are.

- Starting with your toes, squeeze all the muscles as tightly as you can and hold for 5–10 seconds.

- Now, suddenly release the muscles and exhale, feeling the tension disappear.

- Move on to your left leg. Flex your toes upwards and contract your calf muscles. Hold, then release. Now tense the muscles in your thigh. Squeeze, hold and then let go.

- Repeat this on your right leg.

- Work your way up your body, one area at a time: buttocks, abdominals, lower and upper back, shoulders and arms.

- Finally, move on to your face. Clench your jaw, tighten your cheeks, screw up your eyes, wrinkle your forehead. Hold for up to 10 seconds, then suddenly release. Feel the tension melt away.

"In order to relax, it is necessary to let go of all control and surrender to the present moment."

Eckhart Tolle

"Nature does not hurry,

yet everything is

accomplished."

Lao Tzu

Habit-setting

If you've read this far, you will know that happiness results from a series of positive, meaningful behaviours, including gratitude, kindness, self-acceptance, doing activities you love and spending time with others.

But for deep, ongoing happiness, these behaviours need to become habits that shape your day; over time, such small, gradual improvements can prove to be transformative!

Here are some truths about habits.

- It takes on average around 66 days to create a habit.

- A habit is a behaviour that happens on auto-pilot.

- Around 43% of our everyday actions are thought to be habitual. This means they happen while we are thinking about something else, so an awful lot of your life happens without you even noticing. This frees up brain space for other things.

- Habits can be formed both intentionally and unintentionally. This means you can choose to develop a healthy habit just by repeating a positive behaviour.

- Developing a habit requires willpower. We all have willpower.

- With repetition, the behaviour will become second nature.

- Action creates change.

- Change leads to happiness.

"Action may not always bring happiness, but there is no happiness without action."

William James

"Happiness is a choice

that is nourished

by our habits."

Marcus Aurelius

Habit-stacking

Just as it can be tricky to break a bad habit, it can be hard to form a positive one, too. One way you can create a positive habit is through 'habit-stacking'.

Habit-stacking is the art of forming a new habit by attaching it to something you already do. And it's a really effective technique for bringing about a positive change in behaviour.

Here's the idea.

- Choose one positive habit you would like to adopt to increase your happiness.

- Think about one habit you already do on a regular basis.

- Now put the two together.

Here are some examples.

- Every morning, while I wait for the kettle to boil, I will repeat a positive affirmation.

- Every evening, after I've eaten dinner, I will list three things I'm grateful for.

- Every weekend, when I do my grocery shop, I will buy one item to donate to a food bank.

Try thinking about some of your own habits and consider how you could stack them to bring greater happiness into your life.

"Happiness is a habit – cultivate it."

Elbert Hubbard

Drink up

The human body is made up of around 60% water. And while it's possible to go for weeks without food in extremis, we can only survive a few days without water. Drinking plenty of water is therefore essential for our physical health and mental well-being, yet many of us still don't drink enough.

Here are some more reasons to keep a bottle of water handy.

- A lack of water affects the brain, which can lead to a drop in mood.

- Dehydration can also impair your memory and concentration.

- Staying hydrated can stop you gaining weight – it's easy to mistake thirst for hunger, or a sugar craving. So, drinking water can help supress your appetite.

- Drinking water helps keep you regular – we're talking bowels and bladder here. Staying hydrated can also help prevent urinary tract infections – and no one wants one of those!

- It can give you an advantage in the gym or on the pitch – staying well hydrated can boost performance when it comes to sport and exercise.

- Water helps keep your body at a normal temperature – good news if you're prone to hot flushes.

- It helps you move – water lubricates and cushions joints, and it helps protect your spinal cord and other tissues.

"No water, no life.

No blue, no green."

Sylvia Earle

"A drop of water, if it could write out its own history, would explain the universe to us."

Lucy Larcom

Just for fun

In our quest to live a meaningful, contented life, it can be easy to forget the importance of joy. But sometimes you've just got to have fun!

Here are some ideas if you need a giggle.

- Go to a local comedy night.
- Hang out with a hilarious friend.
- Play a silly game, such as charades, Twister or The Floor is Lava.
- Have a blindfold taste challenge.
- Go skinny-dipping.
- Try the ice-bucket challenge.
- Watch – or rewatch – a romantic comedy.

- Watch a silly cat video.

- Hang out with some children. If you don't have your own, perhaps you can borrow some and rediscover your own inner child!

- Have a karaoke night.

- Play a practical joke. Why wait for April Fool's Day?

- Play the game Cards Against Humanity.

- Have a tickle fight.

- Have a pillow fight.

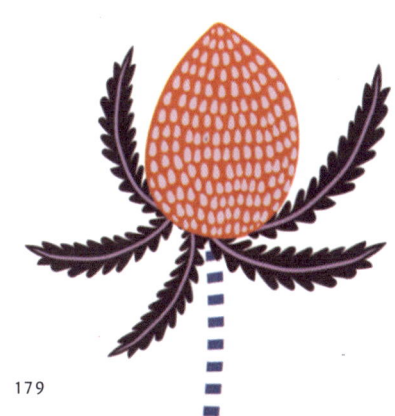

"Laughter is

a sunbeam

of the soul."

Thomas Mann

"The sun is the most
important thing in
everybody's life,
whether you're a plant,
an animal or a fish,
and we take it
for granted."

Danny Boyle

Finding happiness in an unhappy world

Seeking personal happiness can often feel at odds with the suffering in the world. War, climate change, poverty, pollution, disease ... How can we talk about happiness when there is so much tragedy and devastation?

When confronted with world events, it's natural to feel a sense of anxiety, guilt and even despair. However, we can use these feelings as a catalyst for action. What's more, when we make positive changes to our behaviour, we feel more optimistic and empowered. So, in helping others and the planet, we help our own well-being, too.

There are many ways that you can make a difference. Try some of these ideas.

- **Eating kindly** – eating less meat and dairy; buying locally produced, sustainable food.

- **Shopping ethically** – buying second-hand and

fair-trade goods, including clothing; supporting local businesses.

- **Living sustainably** – wasting less; recycling and reusing more.

- **Travelling responsibly** – walking, cycling and using public transport when possible; flying less, or not at all.

- **Supporting charities and aid organisations** – donating money, raising awareness or volunteering.

- **Investing wisely** – using green energy companies and ethical banks.

Although your own actions might seem small and insignificant, there is real power in numbers. Collectively, we can change the world.

"Find the good. It's all around you. Find it, showcase it and you'll start believing in it."

Jesse Owens

"It will never rain roses: when we want to have more roses, we must plant more roses."

George Eliot

Check in with yourself

Now that you are nearing the end of this book, it's a good time to check in with yourself.

These four questions will help you to shine a spotlight on your own happiness.

- What does happiness mean to you?

- What habit-building steps have you taken so far on your happiness journey?

- Where are you on the ongoing road to happiness?

- What are the next steps you need to take to carry on growing and maintaining happiness?

You might like to keep a record of your happiness levels to help you identify the things that make you feel positive and fulfilled – as well as the things that don't. You could use a mood-tracking app, or you could start a happiness journal or scrapbook. You could make notes, draw pictures, or use colours or emojis to represent your mood.

Tracking your emotions can help you to notice how your mood has changed over time, encouraging you to build on those positive habits and to fine-tune your approach. It also allows you to appreciate how far you have come.

Small steps lead to big changes – and that is something that should be celebrated!

"You are enough just as you are."

Meghan Markle

"Smile in the mirror.
Do that every morning
and you'll start to
see a big difference
in your life."

Yoko Ono

And finally ...

Hopefully, this book has inspired you to make time for the things that fill your life with passion, purpose and pleasure – and to practise the habits and qualities that are at the heart of enduring happiness, like gratitude, kindness, optimism, self-acceptance, finding meaning in life, and nurturing human connections and relationships.

To discover genuine happiness is to discover the difference between merely existing and truly flourishing. It takes practice, effort and commitment, but the benefits will flow into your mind, body, thoughts and behaviour, and into the outside world, too.

As you continue your own happiness journey, travel well and may happiness seep like sunshine into every area of your life.

"Everything will be okay in the end. If it's not okay, it's not the end."

John Lennon